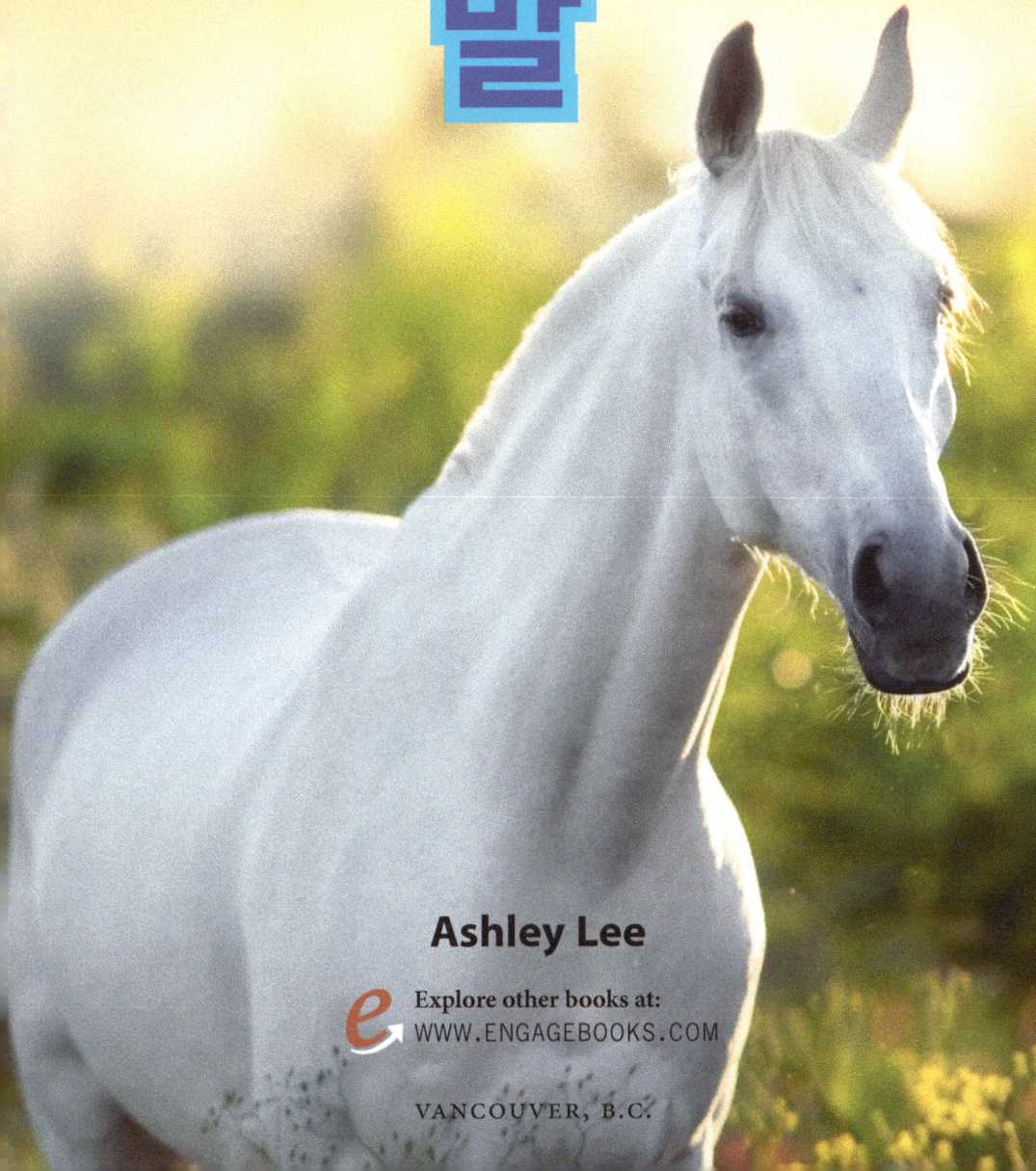

ANIMALS
That Make a Difference!

Horses
말

Ashley Lee

e Explore other books at:
WWW.ENGAGEBOOKS.COM

VANCOUVER, B.C.

e➚ WWW.ENGAGEBOOKS.COM

Horses: Level 1 Bilingual (English/Korean) (영어/한국어)
Animals That Make a Difference!
Lee, Ashley 1995 –
Text © 2021 Engage Books
Edited by: A.R. Roumanis
and Lauren Dick
Translated by: Gio Oh
Proofread by: Tamara Kazali

Text set in Arial Regular.
Chapter headings set in Arial Black.

FIRST EDITION / FIRST PRINTING

LIBRARY AND ARCHIVES CANADA CATALOGUING IN PUBLICATION

Title: Animals That Make a Difference: Horses Level 1 Bilingual (English/Korean) (영어/한국어)
Names: Lee, Ashley, author.

ISBN 978-1-77476-457-2 (hardcover)
ISBN 978-1-77476-456-5 (softcover)

Subjects:
LCSH: Horses—Juvenile literature
LCSH: Human-animal relationships—Juvenile literature

Classification: LCC SF302 .L44 2020 | DDC J636.1—DC23

Contents
목차

What Are Horses?
말은 무엇인가요?

Horses are big, strong animals.
말은 크고 강한 동물이에요.

Horses have lived with humans for thousands of years.
말은 사람과 몇 천년이 넘는 시간을 함께 했어요.

What Do Horses Look Like?
말은 어떻게 생겼나요?

Shires are the tallest horses. They are about 6.6 feet (2 meters) tall. The smallest horses are miniature horses. They are less than 3.3 feet (1 meter) tall.
샤이어 말은 가장 키가 큰 말이에요.
거의 키가 6.6피트(2미터)에요.
가장 작은 말은 미니어처 말이에요.
3.3피트(1미터)보다 작아요.

Horses' feet are protected by a hard nail called a hoof.
발굽이라는 단단한 못으로 말의 발을 보호해요.

Horses have long hair on their necks called a mane.
말의 목에는 갈기라고 불리는 긴 머리카락이 있어요.

Horses have large teeth. A horse's age can be guessed by looking at its teeth.
말은 큰 이빨이 있어요. 이빨을 보고 말의 나이를 예상 할 수 있어요.

Where Do Horses Live?
말은 어디서 사나요?

Many horses live on farms. They sleep in a stable. Some horses live in the wild. They sleep outside.

많은 말들이 농장에서 살아요. 그 말들은 마구간에서 잠을 자요. 몇몇 말들은 야생에서 살아요. 그 말들은 밖에서 잠을 자요.

Clydesdales are large horses that come from Scotland. Hanovarians are strong horses that come from Germany. Paso fino horses comefrom Puerto Rico.

클라이즈데일은 스코트랜드의 큰 말이에요. 하노버리안은 독일에서 온 힘이 센 말이에요. 파소피노는 푸에르토리코에서 온 말이에요.

Scotland
스코틀랜드

North America
남아메리카

Asia
아시아

Atlantic Ocean
대서양

Africa
아프리카

Germany
독일

Puerto Rico
푸에르토리코

Pacific Ocean
태평양

Southern Ocean
남대양

2,000 miles
2,000 마일

4,000 kilometers
4,000 킬로미터

N

Legend 전설
Land 육지
Ocean 바다

9

What Do Horses Eat?
말은 무엇을 먹나요?

All horses eat grass. Horses on farms also eat grain and hay.
모든 말들은 풀을 먹어요. 농장에 있는 말들은 곡식과 건초를 먹기도 해요.

Horses spend up to 17 hours eating grass every day.
말은 매일 풀을 먹으며 하루에 17시간을 보내요.

How Do Horses Talk to Each Other?
말은 서로 어떻게 이야기하나요?

Horses make many different sounds. They will neigh, whinny, or snort. People can tell what horses are feeling by looking at their ears.
말은 여러 소리를 내요. 울거나 낑낑 소리를 내거나 콧소리를 내요. 사람들은 말의 귀를 보고 어떻게 느끼고 있는지를 알 수 있어요.

A horse with its ears back is angry.
귀가 뒤로 넘어가면 말이 화가났다는 뜻이에요.

12

Horses are curious when their ears face forward.
귀가 앞으로 향해있으면 말이 무언가가 궁금하다는 뜻이에요.

Horses often make a snorting sound when they are excited.
콧소리를 내면 말이 흥분했다는 뜻이에요.

Horse Life Cycle
말의 일생

Baby horses are called foals.
아기 말은 망아지라고 불러요.

One-year-old horses are called yearlings.
1살이된 말은 이얼링이라고 불러요.

14

Horses become adults when they are 4 years old.
말은 4살이 되면 어른이에요.

They live for 20 to 30 years.
말은 보통 20년에서 30년을 살아요.

15

Curious Facts About Horses

The fastest known horse ran at a speed of 55 miles (88 kilometers) per hour.
가장 빨랐던 말은 시속 55마일(88킬로미터)의 속도로 달렸어요.

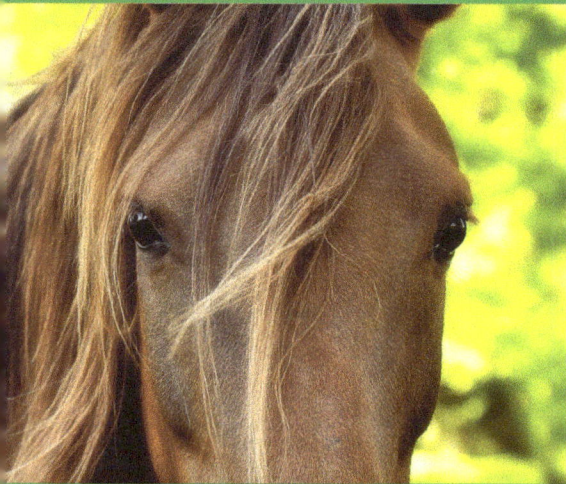

A horse's eyes can see in two different directions at once.
말의 눈은 동시에 다른 두 방향을 볼 수 있어요.

Horses can sleep standing up.
말은 서서 잠을 잘 수 있어요.

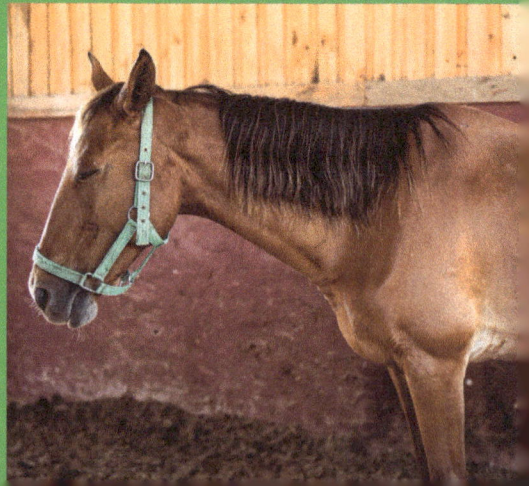

16

말에 대한 흥미로운 사실들

Horses cannot breathe through their mouths. They only breathe through their noses.
말은 입으로 숨을 쉴 수 없어요. 오직 코로만 숨을 쉴 수 있어요.

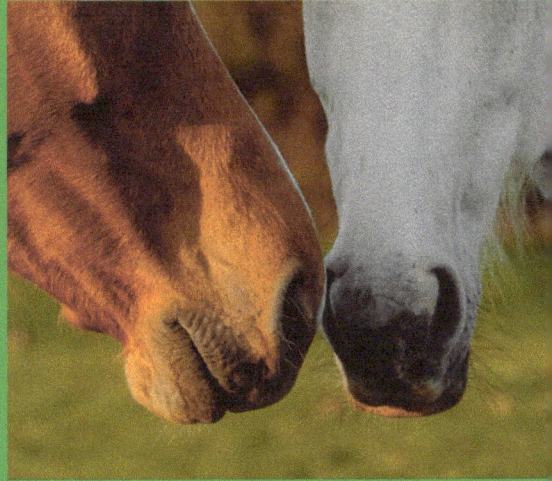

Horses make about 10 gallons (37 litres) of saliva every day.
말은 매일 10갤런(37리터)의 침을 만들어요.

A horse can see behind itself without turning its head.
말은 고개를 돌리지않고도 뒤쪽을 볼 수 있어요.

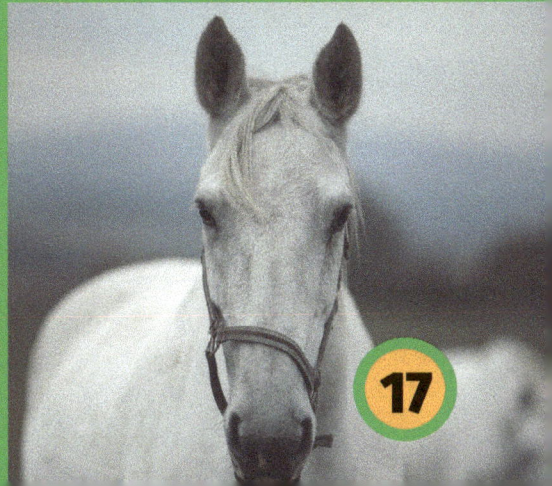

17

Kinds of Horses
말의 종류

Horses are related to zebras and donkeys. There are around 200 different kinds of horses. These are split into three groups.

말은 얼룩말과 당나귀와 관련이 있어요. 약 200종의 말이 있는데 세가지의 그룹으로 나뉘어요.

Draft horses are used for carrying heavy farm loads.
짐수레 말은 무거운 농장의 짐을 나르는데 사용해요.

Light horses are used for riding.
경종마는 승마를 하는데 사용해요.

Ponies are the smallest horses. They are gentle and do not get tired easily.
조랑말은 가장 작은 말이에요. 온순하고 쉽게 지치지 않아요.

19

How Horses Help Earth
말이 지구를 돕는 방법

Many kinds of energy are harmful to Earth.

많은 종류의 에너지들이 지구에 해롭습니다.

20

Horse manure can be turned into energy. This kind of energy does not harm Earth.

말의 거름은 에너지로 사용할 수 있어요. 이런 종류의 에너지는 지구에게 해롭지 않아요.

How Horses Help Other Animals
말이 다른 동물을 돕는 방법

Wild horses break the ice on lakes and rivers in winter.
야생마는 겨울에 호수나 강에서 얼음을 깨뜨려요.

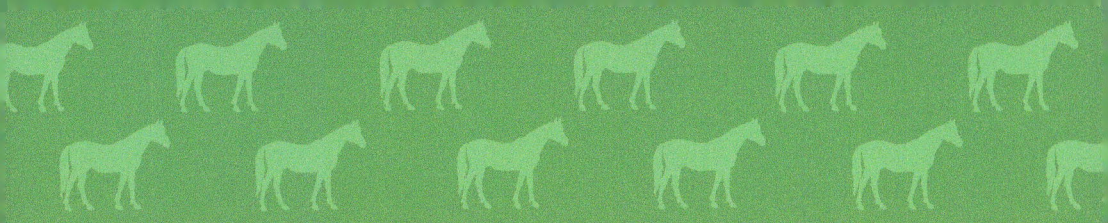

This gives smaller animals a place to drink. Many animals are not heavy enough to break through ice.

작은 동물들에게 물을 마실수 있게 하죠. 많은 동물들은 얼음을 깰 만큼 무겁지 않거든요.

How Horses Help Humans
말이 사람을 돕는 방법

Horses help farmers carry
heavy supplies.
말은 농부들이 무거운 물건을
나르도록 도와요.

Police horses are used in places like Canada. They help keep people safe.
경찰 말은 캐나다 같은 곳에서 사용해요.
사람들을 안전하게 지켜줍니다.

Horses in Danger
멸종위기의 말

Some horses are endangered. This means there are very few of them left.
어떤 말들은 멸종위기에 처해있어요. 말이 거의 남아있지 않다는 뜻입니다.

Dales ponies were once used for carrying heavy loads. They are disappearing because machines are now used to carry heavy objects instead.

데일즈 조랑말은 한때 무거운 짐을 나르는데 사용됐어요. 지금은 기계가 대신하기 때문에 데일즈 조랑말은 점점 사라지고 있어요.

How To Help Horses
말을 돕는 방법

Taking care of horses can cost a lot of money. Owners have to pay for their food and visits from the vet.
말을 돌보는 것은 돈이 많이 들어요. 주인은 수의사와 음식에 대한 돈을 지불해야합니다.

Many people take horse riding lessons to help support horses. This is also a great way to learn more about horses.

많은 사람들이 말들을 돕기위해 승마수업을 받아요. 이것은 말에 대해서 더 많이 배울 수 있는 또 하나의 좋은 방법이에요.

Quiz
새는

Test your knowledge of horses by answering the following questions. The questions are based on what you have read in this book. The answers are listed on the bottom of the next page.

다음 질문에 답하고 말에 대한 지식을 테스트해봐요. 질문은 책의 내용에 기초합니다. 정답은 다음 페이지 하단에 있어요.

1
What is the long hair on a horse's neck called?
말의 목에 있는 긴 털은 무엇인가요?

2
How long do horses spend eating every day?
말은 매일 먹는데 얼마나 시간을 쓰나요?

3
How long do horses live?
말은 얼마나 오래 사나요?

4
What are horses related to?
말은 어떤 동물과 관련이 있나요?

5
What can horse manure be turned into?
말의 거름은 무엇이 될 수 있나요?

6
How do horses help farmers?
말은 농부들을 어떻게 돕나요?

Explore other books in the Animals That Make a Difference series.

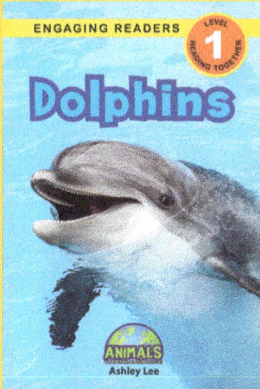

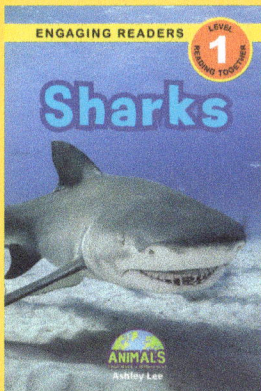

ENGAGING READERS — LEVEL 1 — READING TOGETHER
Bees
ANIMALS
Jared Siemens

ENGAGING READERS — LEVEL 1 — READING TOGETHER
Bats
ANIMALS
Ashley Lee

ENGAGING READERS — LEVEL 1 — READING TOGETHER
Birds
ANIMALS
Ashley Lee

ENGAGING READERS — LEVEL 1 — READING TOGETHER
Dolphins
ANIMALS
Ashley Lee

ENGAGING READERS — LEVEL 1 — READING TOGETHER
Horses
ANIMALS
Ashley Lee

ENGAGING READERS — LEVEL 1 — READING TOGETHER
Ladybugs
ANIMALS
Ashley Lee

ENGAGING READERS — LEVEL 1 — READING TOGETHER
Pigs
ANIMALS
Ashley Lee

ENGAGING READERS — LEVEL 1 — READING TOGETHER
Sharks
ANIMALS
Ashley Lee

ENGAGING READERS — LEVEL 1 — READING TOGETHER
Squirrels
ANIMALS
Ashley Lee

Visit www.engagebooks.com to explore more Engaging Readers.

정답: 1. 갈기 2. 17시간 3. 20살에서 30살 4. 얼룩말과 당나귀 5. 에너지 6. 무거운 물건들을 옮기는 것

Answers: 1. A mane 2. Up to 17 hours 3. 20 to 30 years 4. Zebras and donkeys 5. Energy 6. By carrying heavy supplies